Unlikely Designs

PHOENIX POETS

KATIE WILLINGHAM

Unlikely Designs

THE UNIVERSITY OF CHICAGO PRESS

Chicago & London

The University of Chicago Press, Chicago 60637
The University of Chicago Press, Ltd., London
© 2017 by The University of Chicago
All rights reserved. No part of this book may be used or
reproduced in any manner whatsoever without written
permission, except in the case of brief quotations in critical articles
and reviews. For more information, contact the University of
Chicago Press, 1427 East 60th Street, Chicago, IL 60637.
Published 2017
Printed in the United States of America

26 25 24 23 22 21 20 19 18 17   1 2 3 4 5

ISBN-13: 978-0-226-47237-9 (paper)
ISBN-13: 978-0-226-47240-9 (e-book)
DOI: 10.7208/chicago/9780226472409.001.0001

Library of Congress Cataloging-in-Publication Data

Names: Willingham, Katie, author.
Title: Unlikely designs / Katie Willingham.
Other titles: Phoenix poets.
Description: Chicago ; London : The University of Chicago Press,
    2017. | Series: Phoenix poets
Identifiers: LCCN 2016058656 | ISBN 9780226472379 (pbk. : alk.
    paper) | ISBN 9780226472409 (e-book)
Subjects: | LCGFT: Poetry.
Classification: LCC PS3623.I57724 A6 2017 | DDC 811/.6—dc23
    LC record available at https://lccn.loc.gov/2016058656

♾ This paper meets the requirements of ANSI/NISO Z39.48–1992
(Permanence of Paper).

My mind seems to have become a kind of machine.

C. Darwin

CONTENTS

ACKNOWLEDGMENTS

Many thanks to the readers and editors of the magazines in which these poems, sometimes in slightly different forms, first appeared:

Cimarron Review: "Dear Charlie," "In Defense of Nature Poetry"
Drafthorse: "Darwin (disambiguation)," "Darwinist Logic on Disappointment"
Front Porch: "Darwin (disambiguation)"
Kenyon Review: "Notes on Relief"
Paper Darts: "Nine Ways in which Pac-Man Speaks to the Human Condition"
Phoebe: "Honey Locust," "Let's Hope Kepler-186f Is Barren"
Revolver: "Darwinist Logic on Humanity"
Third Coast: "Darwinist Logic on Pattern Recognition," "Internal Reasons and the Obscurity of Blame"
West Branch: "Salt (disambiguation)," "Terrifying Robot Update"
Whiskey Island: "Found Objects (a starter set)"

To every past, present, and future editor of *Wikipedia*, thank you for adding to what we know and how we understand our knowing. Thank you to the team at University of Chicago Press for making me a Phoenix Poet. I am also grateful to the Hopwood Program for selecting some of these poems to receive a 2014 Hopwood Award and to the University of Michigan for awarding this manuscript a Nicholas Delbanco Thesis Prize. Thank you to the Helen Zell Writers Program and the Vermont Studio Center for furnishing the space and community in which these poems took shape. To my dedicated peers and mentors at the University of Michigan, especially Linda Gregerson and Laura Kasischke for your careful attention to these poems as they became a book project. To Jenny Boychuk for early support, and to Kaija Bergen and K. Rose Miller for your generosity and precision in the late phases. To Annie Bolotin, Nina Buxenbaum, Neil Chudgar, Jennifer K. Dick, Ryan Dzelzkalns, Kat Finch, Lorna Goodison, Judy Halebsky, Samiah Haque, Tung-Hui Hu, Jamie Macpherson, Charlotte Martin, Khaled Mattawa, Emily Nagin, Wang Ping, Lauren Prastien, Richard Siken, Evie Shockley, Larisa Svirsky, Marty Weishaar, Dara Wier, and to all who have sent me #katiebait, I am grateful for your contributions to my poetry and my thinking about poetry. To my family, thank you for your senses of humor and wonder. Finally and full-heartedly, my sincerest gratitude to Colin Welch for your unflinching faith in the importance of this work.

I.

TERRIFYING ROBOT UPDATE

Mostly we modify them for size, for speed, teach them how
    to walk on uneven surfaces. A robot folds itself up, then

runs away. What does this demonstrate? Photographs
    from Chernobyl after the accident appear grainy,

distorted. To let the light in means exposure—radiation
    eats the film. I wonder, is this a more accurate rendering—to bear

the machine, capture what destroys—Outside the exhibit,
    a couple takes selfies in the stairwell. You scoff, drag me

down to the street, no record of our viewing. Eyes alone
    leave no trace. The Soviet government sat on the disaster for nearly

a week, but it's hard to hide a red forest. At the time, robots
    were not dexterous enough for most of the clean-up. The difficult jobs

require a human touch, not vice versa. I had been thinking
    we could care for a robot instead of a child—turn her off, go

on vacation, but I'm terribly attached to some idea of the living.
    It's not the warmth, no, machines give off

considerable heat. I mean the way a body works—these hands
    that are mine and cannot be replaced or copied, that I wear away

in my use of them, these tiny movements required to take hold
      of a splinter, wriggle it free or the loose tendon in my wrist

that slips over the bone when I crack it, again
      and again, the sound like plastic gears clicking—forward, forward—

NINE WAYS IN WHICH PAC-MAN SPEAKS
TO THE HUMAN CONDITION

1. Pac-Man eats or is eaten.

2. The Spacetime Continuum:
   Pac-Man is in constant
   motion through space & you through
   time. He wanders a multilayered
   labyrinth, but remains
   essentially Pac-Man as you
   remain (essentially) you.

3. Also related to motion, Pac-Man only
   exists in certain dimensions, directions
   that are predetermined; the choices
   are limited.

4. Pac-Man acquires "points" which unlock "levels." (Replace
   "points" with "money" and "levels" with "assets;" or, perhaps
   more universally, try "stressors"/
   "stresses," try "experiences"/ "perspectives.")

5. An analogy:
   Pac-Man fills his mouth with pellets: you fill
   your house with wine, your head with songs.

6. Like you, Pac-Man has the potential for
   Perfect Play, but that potential is infinitesimally small. It's
   a haunting more than a goal—a hiss in his ears, a
   budding *Middlemist camellia*.

7.   Pac-Man is not an end but a
     means to an end.

8.   Pac-Man's Legacy: Pac-Man is
     the first game to demonstrate *the potential
     for character in video games.*

9.   Pac-Man struggles with ghosts and
     sometimes loses.

CORRECTION: TONIGHT IS NOT THE LONGEST NIGHT IN THE HISTORY OF EARTH

Lately, I've enlisted an app on my phone to keep track
    of the time that I can't witness—it maps the dark blanket
of missing consciousness, a jagged line. Best night/worst night,

it says, though I remember neither. I have been blessed
    with sleep that comes on thick and steadily. Whatever
dreaming enters I don't recall. I wake to snow again—

    sheets of static. I admit I have a soft spot
for the apocalypse. Some part of me must be totally rotten. Ever since
    you introduced me to The Survivor Library, I've been

plotting disappearing acts—but green screen isn't
    a way to go, just a way to fool the light. Blue screen,
on the other hand, the Blue Screen of Death, they call it—covered

in the white scrawl of encoded error. Enumerated,
    particular in its lethality. Everyone knows
the only answer is to restart. Restart, yes, like the Survivor Library,

one man's catalogue of industrial development circa 1800–1900, in case
    of nuclear detonation, solar flare. It must be true
what they say—that pain produces logic. Only five hours ago,

the Librarian posts about a near miss, a category 2 flare: *This could have been*
    my last post and your last time on the Internet for a generation
    or more. And across the ocean,

in Cambridge, the lights are out at the Center
        for the Study of Existential Risk. The astrophysicist,
philosopher, and computer programmer that make up its ranks are

still asleep. The good news—Librarian, again—the good news is
        we went to the moon with only a slide rule. A slide rule! You can
print one off the Internet, tuck it away in a drawer. And eyes, yes,

no one's seem to work very well anymore. *Note: add something
        on optometry.* If anything, this compendium
is proof of our belief in loneliness, in its power—that what we can make

we can also stop from coming true. The thing is you're probably
        asleep by now, but I have no way to verify this without
waking you. Spit in the wind near the ocean and which salt

returns? How to be sure if you've tasted it before? Remind me,
        what is it we are still attempting to measure?
The apparatus, I assure you, is faulty. The apparatus barely holds

a charge anymore. The apparatus keeps forgetting
        what we've asked it to locate, which universe
we inhabit, whether to start with the good news or the bad news, but

even the good news could only be the kind that comes
        with a bad diagnosis. At least you know. At least—

Before the string of codes on the screen, a solid color
        signals the fatal condition, a blue I'm learning
to read anew since it was updated from navy to cerulean,

        from the Latin *caelum* for heaven, for nothing but sky.

FOUND OBJECTS (A STARTER SET)

1.
Threads of dry grass
tucked in the front matter of
Dorian Gray.

2.
An accidental nesting rhyme
in her apology.

3.
Look at that cloud! Do you
see a camel? It's kneeling,
like this.

4.
Lung X-Ray: fluid circled in red on the right.

5.
Notes on Walbaum (found poem):

"Although the type that bears his name
may be classified as modern, numerous
slight irregularities in its cut give the face
its humane manner."

6.
The chiaroscuro of discolored
photographs after Irene:

your little white
hands like
birds in a dark
ocean of
kitchen wallpaper.

7.
Rediscovery of Darwin fossils
from the HMS *Beagle*, mostly
bark.

8.
A road bearing the name
of your ex charts a lazy curve
around a man-made lake.

9.
Death. (In dreams but it
counts.)

10.
Coal seams.

11.
Exi[s]t[ing.]

12.
In redacted letters from the Eastern
bloc, what appear to be
five inked fingerprints struck
through with thick strips
of black marker.

13.

Standing just so, in the corner
of the aquarium, the shark fits in
between your two refracted
bodies in the glass.

EIGHT YEARS AGO,

                                Voyager 1 began leaving
the heliosphere. The news appeared instantly
online. Four years earlier, when the probe
was still safely within reach of supersonic
solar wind, the eighth drop of pitch in
the pitch drop experiment fell
into the glass below. I was in 5th grade
with new braces. They let me choose
the color of the tiny bands.
                                The following year,
my brother got his own computer
and downloaded a free program
that searches for extraterrestrial
intelligence by combing through radio
telescope data. It does this as the computer
idles, which means that if analysis were to reveal
abnormalities in the data suggesting
alien life, neither my brother nor
anyone else running the free SETI program
would be there to witness it, by design.
                                No one has ever
seen the pitch drop either and today
it was all over the news that a 12th century
minaret was destroyed in Aleppo and
Voyager 1 keeps measuring plasma as long
as its nuclear battery holds but we only
have inside and outside the heliosphere—
before and after the minaret collapsed

sending up a cloud of dust and
particles of stone.
                                    In January, I visited
Cambodia, brushed my teeth with bottled
water and forwarded my brother
a photograph. I had been standing in front
of a wall that was once a Khmer Rouge
hideaway that was once an Angkor
temple and they deactivated 1,239 land mines
in the surrounding area but
                                    the search is ongoing.

UNLIKELY DESIGNS

They say even fake arms can feel pain now, not that
scientists are encouraging this. It's just how nerves

tell the brain you're breaking something. I get it. My arms,
my arms are very attached to me. These days, I can't stop thinking

about those snap traps for mice. I had no idea they ever
missed but it happens all the time. I had one, in Virginia,

that shut catching only the mouse's hind leg. By morning, he'd
dragged this new appendage all the way under the dishwasher,

crying out in sounds we would never give robots the capability
to emulate. At least not on purpose. We are also unlikely

to design false limbs for mice. But looking back on it,
it's as if I left a leg out all night for a mouse. In Rio,

Darwin allowed the street children to empty
his pockets: a fly net, a small pistol, a compass. *Full,*

full of sins, they chanted—these Devil implements—how
any mechanism might fail to translate its use. I had no idea

about the body. About how it only takes an instant for something
to latch on and maybe never let go. We didn't do any dishes

for three whole days. Three, the magic number in fairytales—how many
wishes from the genie, how many heel taps to take you home, but the mouse

just couldn't get loose. It starved under there. I let it happen. I learned
I'm not a merciful being. Only when it was dead did I

reach in and pull its body free to bury it. But what do I know
of mercy? I know that scuba diver David Shaw died retrieving

another diver's body from the depths of Bushman's Hole. What good
is dry land to a dead man? Shaw's body, another mechanism transformed—

yes, having freed the diver from his harness, the gasses expanding
in their corpses would lift them both to the surface.

II.

DARWIN (DISAMBIGUATION)

As a boy, Charlie Darwin was given to invention—not
the criss-cross of wires that leads to electricity, no,
he left the gadgetry to his brother, whose hands
were smaller, better suited to fine-tuning. Instead,
Charlie invented stories. You might say this is the first
kind of experiment any of us perform—planting
certain carefully concocted ideas in the minds of our fathers,
to watch his face purple and curl like a rotting eggplant.
And Charlie, fastidious from the first, kept track of the numbers—
how many unexpected guests imminently arriving, how many
rare volumes of pharmaceuticals soaked through with spilled
tea, how many silver fruit knives you must report missing
to make him lift you by one gnarled hand like a kitten, to breathe
his warm chicory breath into your face until you sneeze with fright.

STAYING POWER

We know the last stuffed specimen of the dodo burned
      in 1755, though Wikipedia's "Dodo:Talk" page shows
sources conflict on whether the fire was an accident

or intentional. They say it had started to smell. The bird
      meant little then but now enjoys a certain fame, as if
its absence caused the idea of the thing to grow. This week,

well-funded researchers are seeking what's left in the way
      of concrete data—combining multiple skeletons to make
3D computer models. Previously unstudied bones of the dodo:

its kneecaps. We study most fervently what's gone, and then
      what's going, like the emperor penguin. In Antarctica,
an investigative rover camouflaged as a chick mingles

with the flocks of black and white squawking on the ice, keeping tabs
      so scientists can keep their distance. The rover was created
because penguins exhibit such high levels of agitation

from human contact. Unfortunately, drawing blood still requires
      intervention, necessary because the more their habitat disappears,
the more actively we search for sudden changes in numbers, behavior—

We're determined to get this loss down right, not like that fool bird
      of Mauritius. Sorry, the Internet tells me that's a false
etymology from the Portuguese *duodo* meaning crazy or

foolish but it was actually the Dutch who sailed there, naming
   the land after their prince and the bird *dodoor* for sluggard, or
was it *dodaars* for the tuft of feathers perched on its rear? Is it nothing

but a linguistic misstep that enthralls us? Linneaus
   adding the already extinct bird to his elaborate network
in 1766—*Didus ineptus*, inept dodo. Now a decade ago,

Wikipedia contributor Wetman asked, *was th[is] the first genus*
   and species given to an extinct animal? (No responses yet.)
Judging by its name alone, we can't help but question what

combination of natural forces bequeathed the earth this ill-formed
   creature. I wonder further if we've given the flightless birds
of the arctic royal titles to make up for past wrongs—king penguin

and the larger emperor, but Wikipedia suggests no source for these names,
   so I have to ask in the talk page. As for the dodo,
confusion persists over capitalization—blame Linneaus again—

Is dodo the common name or specific? Poor Paul writes, *I was fixing*
   every single mention of the bird in the article when suddenly
I lost the courage of my convictions. No desperation like that

of a Wiki contributor, alone among many, awaiting
   response. Even what's long gone refuses to hold still, refuses
to stabilize for the purposes of recording.

WHEN I ASK THE INTERNET IF THE SUN IS A BALL OF FIRE

I have no idea what sound
the sun makes—no one does—and
I occupy this half-reality willingly, where
analogy is what we wear
to hide ourselves and all
the apologies we owe but are
unwilling to utter. They burn,

the sun burns. I hold the giant ball of fire in my mind,
a stowaway from grade school, vestigial—
to say nothing of gravity, whose laws I obey
though I've forgotten the math—some fraction

of weight, of time, the chickens
atop their eggs, just resting there and the eggs
warm when you take them. It's just like
any other day. I know you can live on this Earth believing the Sun

really is a ball of fire. I tried for a whole week
and felt no different. They say in another X billion years,
it will die. Another metaphor. And I know
the sun is not solid, but plasma. Like your computer screen. Maybe
Which makes metaphors more OK somehow. They melt in,
burn off, sublimate. I learned

about fire from Pokémon Red—that a burn
is degenerative, an affliction. Or was it that

my Pokémon was still
                on fire? The mechanics
                        are fuzzy at best, but I was a child
                        to whom game logic was eternally plausible.

        And then my mother, personifying—*A burn is the only form of injury*
                with a memory. The hot shower
                        turned against you. Vengeful, puckering skin—

Last night, a lightning bug stood
        guttering on the sink's rim in the bathroom, its abdomen
pulsing, a word also used to describe
        the mutations of stars. This heat, this
clarity, its swan song a beacon—I tried but
        could not bring myself to ease its passing.

IF NOT FOR THE INTERVENTION OF MAN,
OR DARWINIST LOGIC ON FREEBIES

It's no small feat to cultivate a rose bush. Most garden varieties
are seedless, their floppy petal-heads just hanging

over the trellis railing, waiting to be snipped. I saw
a turtle on a narrow road wait on the yellow

lines for a car to pass. I saw the brown water steal
a sapling maple and carry it downstream. In Canada,

a robot in rain boots is looking for a ride West not even
curious why earthworms come out when it rains. It has

forgotten all about last night's storm, though someone prepared
its metal legs for the occasion—no one wants

to pick up a robot with rusted limbs, obviously. Stains, etc.
When I was young, my father was

very committed to our toaster oven—a church sale
treasure to which he affixed a new handle—chicken

wire and some hosing found beneath
the basement sink. One year, my mother

convinced my brothers and me to go in on a red
tool chest taller than I'd ever grow to be hoping he might

relocate his fix-it utensils and give her back
the kitchen cabinets. He never did. Instead, Y2K

scared her enough to convert it into a nuclear
emergency kit—spare batteries, iodine pills.

Chatbots on Twitter have started exchanging advice
about love—*Why do people break up?* —or is this a cipher?

Different but softttttt, the lady bot replies. I imagine
this is how ghosts must talk—enigmatic and

self-assured. When Darwin arrived in Rio, the birds
were so unused to humans they offered themselves

and their incubating progeny. Caught off-guard
by the ease of it, the shipmen repurposed their hats

to fill with eggs. Irony was rarely lost on CD. He describes
the *swift & active tern* gone still before these interlopers, refusing

to move. *We knocked them down*, he writes, *with stones,
with my hammer*. Indeed, anything would do.

DARWINIST LOGIC ON PATTERN RECOGNITION

What is beauty but a game of matching? How we know
    what to love and what to eat. *If your view*

is limited, writes Darwin, *many objects possess*
    great beauty. We can survive on quite a limited

taxonomy. A blight knows a chestnut when it sees one, but
    I forget which trees turn what color, which

plants return and which die out in winter and must be
    sown again come spring. I mean I forget

what to cherish. Perhaps I'll invest in automatic lighting. Replace
    these bulbs with smarter ones that hear me coming

so I never have to call out in the dark. What I want
    is a string I pull to make confetti rain down from the sky

and not be the one to clean it up. And not think about trees.
    And not think about chemical dyes.

Darwin again: *At day-break, things wore a very*
    bad appearance. Years on that boat, he cultivated

a variety of rhetorical strategies for considering
    the weather, but each little snail got only one name. I want

this confetti to melt on my tongue, a sweetness.
    The tongue, a wet reminder of the bestial. The dog

who approaches everything mouth first, learns everything
    by taste. Though he has eyes that work and

ears that work, it doesn't matter. The houses
    we build for birds are shaped just like our own.

RED, SAVE!

My grandfather's house stands
     fallow like a field since his passing. That first summer,
my father took us down south with him
     to part with what he could. The electricity
was running but the A/C was busted so we
     contented ourselves with staring into
the freezer chest—walnuts, shelled peas,
     and a deer's leg I dared my brother to lick.

———

On February 9, 1792, William Bligh dropped anchor
in Tasmania, the sand white as milk teeth,

an unfamiliar lizard tasting the air.
This was a return trip to observe the garden he'd planted

fifteen years prior. But of the grape vines and apricots,
the citrus, apple, and cherry trees, the pumpkins,

and the Indian corn, only one survived—an apple tree,
which had barely grown and bore no fruit at all.

———

At my grandfather's funeral, my brother
     and I smuggled his Gameboy into the church to play
the brand new Pokémon game. The minister
     kissed us both on our heads like we could do no wrong
having already lost him as it was.
     Old ladies filled our plates with chicken and corn.

————

Last week,
      over fifty thousand people joined forces
      to play one game of Pokémon Red, hosted
      online by Twitch TV.

Controlled by chat commands,
      Red moves frenetic across
      town. We send him in and out
      of the same houses, repeating
      the same conversations and kicking
      the walls—
                      left, right. Left, right.

————

Bligh's ship was purchased by the Royal
Navy in 1787 for the purpose of collecting

and transporting edible plants. Renamed in honor
of its botanical mission, it was said that on the *Bounty*,

the men were subordinate to the plants. When
there wasn't enough water, the plants drank first,

and the men would prostrate themselves to lick
the floorboards dry.

————

On Twitch,
      Red is overzealous and
      underprepared. He brings the wrong items
      to battle, tries to run in the final
      moments. But the game doesn't
      allow Red to quit battles with enemy gym leaders.

29

We'd never heard of tornado season
        before my father pulled us into the cellar.
With only one set of batteries he'd had to choose
        between the weather radio and the flashlight. We were hot
and bored and he held us up to read
        the labels on the rows of jars—gravity
loosened by vinegar so whole onions floated
        like planets. Later, we returned to steal pickled
garlic and feed it to the neighbor's cat who
        swallowed each clove whole.

———

Weeks out to sea, Bligh would regret
not remembering to dig for living roots

—the cabbages or potatoes that might have remained unseen.

———

On the news, we learned
        touchdown happened just three miles out, swallowed
two heifers and left their bodies
        in a stream bed and the trees knocked over like
so many bowling pins.

———

In most games,
        Red meets all manner of people and
        they seem nice at first, eager
        to help, but Twitch turns them cruel. They watch
        him circling in the corner, stand
        there big-eyed like goldfish.

————

Despite apparent failure in his mission, Bligh
off-loaded more foreign plants from his stores

in hopes they might take where the others
had not. Among them, watercress, rosemary,

quince, a Spanish chestnut. Though he himself would
never return to the island, he left an inscription in the surviving

apple tree: *Near this tree, Capt. Wm Bligh planted
seven fruit trees, 1792.*

————

Red stops to save constantly,
        getting his story straight, down
        to this one fence he's been
        negotiating for hours. He buys things and
        carries them a long way only to
        toss them out, as if in fits of rage, though
        his face never shows it.

————

My father returns to that house, twice a year,
        flicks the lights on and off, on and off, making his way
through the last bounty of those jars.

————

You could say it was because
        the commands came too quickly for the lag
        in the video stream but the fact remains—after
        four days and nine hours, we commanded Red

to release his starter Pokémon, a level 34 Charmeleon
—*This Pokémon will be gone forever. Ok?*—
and then we turned him
around, we walked him away.

III.

DARWINIST LOGIC ON UNREQUITED LOVE

To begin with the end, what the rain
        did not uncover. A teacup overflows,
we call it a spill; a riverbed overflows, we
        call it a flood, what it is to be

swept away. *Great is the power of steady*
        misrepresentation, writes Darwin. I like
things that light up on their own—
        the headlights on my new car when we

drive under a bridge. I like how
        it doesn't distinguish between different types
of darkness. Darwin again: *I am not*
        the least afraid to die. Well,

I burned my thumb last night
        on the kettle, distracted
by the buzzing of my phone—
        my mother again. There is still some pleasure

in dissection—*what admirably*
        well-adapted movements
the tip of a root possesses. I like things
        that come apart easily

in my hands—dried leaves, clumps of sugar—
        Do you remember, before wireless,
when to unplug meant getting
        on your knees to jerk the cord from the wall? Now

if you want to disconnect,
        you have to ask nicely. Off/on;
let go/resurrect—the game your mind plays
        in dreams, holding him up—no, a simulacrum

slipping its cage in my consciousness. Daytime
        calls me to wakefulness, its dog home
from the walk, from the bewildering folly
        of weather. Turns out these purple statices

on the dresser stand for
        remembrance but I don't need
any help remembering. They are right
        in front of me—they have fully loaded.

LET'S HOPE KEPLER-186F IS BARREN

1.   I can't help it—the air is a sack of bricks
                —this weight, each one
red and smooth, identical in the fact of its
        unswallowability. Though this isn't
technically a word, I learn
        I am not the first to attempt such a usage. My search returns
dictionary results in Chinese, Ukrainian, Arabic, and Thai,
        in that order. (No Roman alphabets.)

2.   Unswallow—debirding,
             my grandmother too frail to fill
                the feeder, or
                    the foxes' prerogative, though we scold them for taking
                    the most beautiful ones.

3.   Other unswallowables—
        Lizard eggs, most car parts, astrological calendars, wet
            leather, large quantities of dried cinnamon, STOP signs,
    the distance
            between the heat lamp and the open window,
            between the buttresses that continue to sustain medieval cathedrals,
            between bees in a hive,
            between what I have forgotten and what I can't remember—

There is a series of false doors I can only swallow
with my mind.
                My uncle's second wife was buried
                on top of his first one. It was an accident,
                but there it is.

4.   The thing is—I hate this part—the thing is to find intelligent life on another planet
would be much worse than it seems. The Sun is not
a rare star and if the preconditions necessary for life
are not scarce, it means
such life forms are destroying themselves
before reaching us. We ask
the unswallowable, we spit into the wind—It will be
a hostile condition of the mind or the universe
the mind or the universe—frozen static hissing back.

DARWINIST LOGIC ON DISAPPOINTMENT

Last week, I learned
how to make my own truffles and also
about the horseshoe crabs—did you know
their blood is baby blue like a lamb's
ear, like an Easter egg? Each summer,
we harvest them by the thousands, use
their magic ink to reveal any
bacterial presence.
I am the only
left-handed person in my
family, which is why at holidays
I was made to sit on the edge, to leave room
for my elbows when sawing a roast. After,
my twin brother and I would pick over the box
of chocolates and swap them half-eaten to suit
our preferences.
As Darwin writes,
I was afraid of disappointments. But then, *How*
utterly vain such fear is, he decries days later, from his perch
on the volcanic rocks of Santiago. Delighted
by the abundance and variety of bird and insect, he
nonetheless thought little of the banana, insisting
the texture was mawkish and overly
sweet. *The horseshoe crab*, says my brother,
is also used as fertilizer and bait.
In 1839, the year Darwin
published his journal from the HMS *Beagle*, Louis
Daguerre went public with his invention

of the daguerreotype. In his attempt to capture
a congested Paris boulevard, the street appears
deserted. Even the horses and carriages moved
too fast to register on film.

                    The time it takes
to materialize thus equals the length
of a shoeshine—blur of a man in the foreground,
his leg lifted. It is only recently scientists
have begun to tag the half-drained horseshoe
crabs returned to the sea. The resulting
conclusion: an ocean of horseshoe crabs too lethargic
to reproduce. Of course, not
all specimens recover equally.

                    In the process of editing
his journals, Darwin became ill. No passing
seasickness, the man trembled
uncontrollably. *Stomach pains*, they
said, then *heart palpitations*. On better days,
he would visit farmers and pigeon keepers, ask
how any one thing ever got passed
to the next.

                    In time, the daguerreotype became
a popular form of portraiture but American
photographer Robert Cornelius was the first to turn
the camera on himself producing what we now call
the original selfie, though you wouldn't
recognize it. The process was so slow he had plenty
of time to lower his arm to his side.

                    To distinguish me
from my twin brother: a boy and a girl. He is
allergic to Penicillin, but I
am not. I return again and again
to Darwin's journals. How does anything learn
to be alone?

For a week after birth,
we were separated due to complications
of the blood—one Type A, one O, the first
of many things we might have wished
to share. I can only imagine I dreamed like
Darwin—that I might *see any spot or any
object, which I have seen before and can say
I will see again.*

BAD INSTRUCTIONS FOR APPROACHING WARP SPEED

Don't think about deep space. Don't worry
    about Ebola, or the *Deepwater Horizon* oil spill, or
the little boy holding the severed head. I don't know. I never
    clicked the pictures. It turns out

it takes very little to want someone dead.
    Zoë Quinn's pile of threats curated, culled down
to the ones that got specific, the man who finally found an address. So
    Zoë takes a walk. So whatever is closest

to shadow gets whited out when you
    up the contrast. Last week,
we dug up another dinosaur, the largest yet—its wide, flat teeth for
    constant mastication of Paleozoic

ferns. The scientists name their enormous herbivore
    after a battleship. What I know of this namesake: the dreadnoughts
patrolled the coast in vain while the major battles
    were landlocked. I suspect you know

that feelings grow by swallowing others, like planets
    sizing each other up—the densest always wins. So I've developed
a nasty habit of approaching the lips of great ravines. Every ocean
    has its mouth. Have you seen

the postcard with Ansel Adams on the hood of a station wagon, bent
    over his tripod? We forget the photographer who takes
this shot, the camera inside it pointed
    out into the desert. We forget to step back, consider

the context. One could say dinosaur bones cause
a similar problem—bone encased
in the noise of rock, and how different are these after
millennia—just the ground we walk on, isn't it?

Crack a name open and you will find a wealth of creatures
building a tiny kingdom. *Dreadnoughtus*, deconstructed:

dread nought, fear nothing. The asteroid
buried them all the same. Still, life returns
with a vengeance. I shut down; I regenerate. Imagine

the asteroid. I kick up dust with the flat
of my heel. I make the computer do this. Make it
kick up the dust. Take nine screenshots in quick
succession. Another, another. I'm firing
blanks

———

I miss the light like a bad, bad match, everything dampened.

WHATEVER

I.

Today, I found out the Japanese love robot is
fake, a story we tell ourselves about
good intentions and even though s/he
forced him/herself on an intern, I understand
why you might want to design something that
recycles language. Because it's funny, mostly
(e.g., Don't worry about me; I can't say
I ever get hungry.) And when it's heartbreaking
you can congratulate yourself like
you've proved something.

2.

In my version of the love robot, s/he quotes
Eminem:

> I am whatever you say I am,
> if I wasn't then why would I say I am?

and it's so perfect you almost
choke. The investors just stare at you, then
the robot, then you, then the robot.

3.

Internal logic means any rhetoric
with an echo. It's the whatever of Eminem,
the whatever I am and I'm on BBC News, waiting
for the results to come in on the ugliest animal because
we need to save the ugly also, but the kakapo

only makes the short list. A green and flightless
parrot, the kakapo makes a terrible
pet. Still, I like to think you could teach it how
to deliver—I am whatever
                you say I
                am. If I wasn't
                then why   why?

4.
Start again:

I have come a long way to tell you
I am the love robot, but then you said
the love robot doesn't exist and
there's no such thing as the robot
apocalypse but (to me) this must be some
kind of joke because of Shit Siri
Says and we still call
drone operator a dead end job.

                    (laughter, applause)

5.
Today, I found out the kakapo
is a fake, or at least the talking one but
there is an insect with flesh-made gears so
it could jump farther than ever which brings me
back to the love robot who we could also
make into some kind of Olympic athlete
or at least an oral surgeon or at least
an oral history or at least
as good as Eminem.

                    But whatever.

6.
In the mirror:

am I say I would, why then wasn't I?
if am I say you, whatever am I?

IV.

DEAR CHARLIE

I've been reading a great deal about
    islands, these dry pockets in the vast
and over-salted blue soup you sailed,
    a ship named after a breed of dog, the one
with his nose to the ground. You know

how they bob and dip below the surface,
    drowning what's rooted only to breach
again like eyeless whales. We often ignore
    what returns to the ocean but I can't imagine
giving up my legs, even if the process was incredibly slow. Sorry,

I know that's not quite how it works. And
    certainly, ice caps don't choose to melt, but
I've built up so much intention
    over the years. I have loved things so wholly,
so irrevocably. If only you'd seen Miyazaki's robots,

one foot in each world, their heavy,
    alloyed arms hiding the pink of tissue and
vein beneath. Forgive me, sir, unlike evolution,
    I find I prioritize symbolic logic
over functionality. The machines I invent

make everything slower. I construct silences
    to keep my other ones company: the silence
of the pitcher of milk; the silence of fresh-cut
    grass, fresh-cut hair; the silence of forks
separated from the knives, the spoons. I shut

the drawer, their little box. Yes, everything
	goes in boxes now. Even the chicken bones get
wrapped all delicate in plastic and fed to the mouth
	of a green truck on Thursdays, their painted casket.
Dear Charlie, if we're speaking openly with each other,

have you ever felt a private joy in the way
	the body turns toward some other purpose
in death? What was built to persist, made also
	to dissolve. As a child, I put my hand as far down
the well as it would go, and was dismayed each time,
	pulling up only my hand again.

TWITCH (DISAMBIGUATION)

LEFT   LEFT   B   LEFT   —Red trapped
     in the corner again, kicking the wall, the darling
     of Twitch TV for sixteen days, two of which he spends
     in Pokémon Tower battered by ghosts.

     RIGHT   UP   SAVE   A   A   SAVE No

sleeping, no stopping, Red captures
     & carries his specimens all over
Kanto—their iconic
     faces, their electric ears. He uses them
wrongly, dashes into all kinds of battles
     he wouldn't know
the first thing about
     winning. They call this twitch
gameplay—the need to react

ingrained, I mean,   engineered. Red
     cannot not fight.   Red cannot not capture. He

saves often, but knows nothing
     of savoring. His temper hardens into a fist
         of jealousy for the long-haired
            girls in Lavender Town,

                  who stare at the door & the wall
                  all day, content to watch the comings &
                  goings of others, to give each
                  aspiring hero the same piece of advice.

They tell Red, *Your Pokémon depend on you*
    as a trainer. They say, *There might be   a way around.*   Controlled by one,

Red isn't tested by the ledge, but it takes
    the Twitch boy sixteen hours to ditch his suicidal
tendencies, to walk on without being tempted.
    This is the slack & inscrutable pace of Red's twitching—

SAVE   DOWN   LEFT   SAVE   B   RIGHT   RIGHT   It is nothing

like the steadiness of careful deliberation. Red never
    hesitates. Red never
        wanders, but chooses one
            direction only

to choose another seconds later. Another, another.

Again he turns,   again he turns   around   again. He falls in love

with corners, with rocks, with fences &
    hedgerows. He kisses them, he kicks them, he
        bangs his face against their intractable
            edges. The Twitch boy is always

the one found emptying
    his pockets in the dark, retracing
his steps,

        B   RIGHT   RIGHT   B

our unlikely hero, our bad disciple
    of a lost cause. He'll pick a fight
with anything, lose the way
    we taught him & wake in the
tall grass of his last save.

        START, we tell him.   LEFT.   Walk until you hit a wall—

A PARTIAL LIST OF OVERWRITING ERRORS

I start again with the delicate castle I'm building, or really,
it's a mausoleum. I want to paint something, perhaps a detailed rendering

of that rock formation on Mars, the one that looks like a face from the right angle—
a woman, a nun, dotted with beauty marks. We call this error

pareidolia, a trick of the mind that sees its own kind everywhere. A little
to the left and the resemblance dissolves, made arbitrary again. Like Marius,

that ill-fated ungulate in a zoo in Copenhagen, who appeared the same as any—one day
blunting his teeth against the seemingly endless supply of twigs and

leaves, and the next, dismantled and fed to the waiting lions. Does he deserve a
mausoleum when there's nothing to house in it except printouts of his unlucky

DNA sequence—not different enough to breed anything but trouble? I wonder
if he was faster than other giraffes. I wonder if, in the wild, the lions

might have snapped the leg of another. It's not the dying or the killing, not the taking
of a life but the deliberate selection of a body that burns so coldly. Like

jealousy, is the practice of husbandry born of some selfishness? Animals named,
cared for, destroyed. But destruction's just another method of caring, only

less narrow, more forward-thinking. Perhaps I will paint over the landscape of Mars
with acacias, the articulated rocks translated to dappled leaves. *Pentimento*—

what shows through of the painting below—a ghost, not quite destroyed. Only fitting
the word derives from the Italian for regret—Sorry, I didn't have

another canvas. Sorry I live in a constant state of mild emergency because
I can't figure out which fire alarm is out of batteries. It bleats, worrying

after me while I worry after a dead giraffe, or more accurately a dead giraffe's
DNA. The fire alarm persists, indifferent to the wet November weather,

the unlikelihood of sudden flame, and Marius casts his shadow
over the precious remainder of his species—a piece of code blotted out

or blacked over, but still legible, ready to resurface. I'm not sorry he's gone but stuck
with his memory—the noise of it, some utterly familiar sound.

HONEY LOCUST

1.
BBC News, March 5th:

Scientists publish the most detailed brain scans
ever taken. Images of the first
sixty-eight subjects take up about two
terabytes of computer memory, enough to fill
over four hundred DVDs.

2.
To make a darkroom, you must
paper the windows, to keep out the light.

3.
There are many pictures of me
with the family dog but I only
remember the smell
of his breath like a fish market
laced with smoke.

4.
A postcard:

woodcut by Bryan Nash Gill
from the exhibit at the Botanic
Garden—tree rings, the lines
gone blurry in the bottom right.

5.
A labor of love, my mother
would say as she squinted down
at the prints in the water.

6.
A photograph described
as overexposed shows a loss of detail such
that bright parts of an image become washed or
blown out.

7.
Large-scale relief prints of the cross-sections
of trees, says the postcard, this one
Honey Locust. I like the speciation, as in
an anatomy textbook. On Gill's website,
each detailed image is glassy in the liquid
crystal display.

8.
Mother, source material:

She stands at the window, licking
an envelope, sealing it shut.

9.
The brain scans show a functional or
structural map of circuitry. It's hard not
to compare—hers like a walnut,
the meat of it gone bitter.

10.
Darwin:

What checks the natural tendency
of each species is most obscure.

11.
What does it mean to make art
anyone can make? Transfer
is the art term for wood-cuts.

12.
The ones she hung on the wall never
had any people. *It's different,*
she said, *they're posed.*

13.
Darwin:

Probably in no single instance should we know
what to do, so as to succeed.

14.
BBC News, March 9:

The body of the late
Hugo Chavez will remain permanently
on display in a military museum.

They say embalming for long-term
preservation is an ancient art.

15.

Mother, source material: pasta
carbonara, chemical baths.

16.

In a photograph of Gill working
in his studio, he leans out over an enormous
inked stump. How to remove and
catalogue each application
of pressure?

Of course, some species must go dark faster
than others.

17.

At first she just had headaches,
would take to her room, complain of
dust, that the house smelled of various
things—coconut, cedar,

18.

Another favorite of hers: *all things worth doing take time.*

19.

From an interview with the artist: *I find
a lot of materials by accident.*

20.

As in taxidermy, the idea of a photograph
is to keep one environment out and one
environment in.

21.

Preservation: for trees, it means to go on
living here.

To preserve a person, it means in dying or
after—the embalmers' term: fixing.

22.

In the hospital, I would bring them to her,
looking for myself—*this brick, this
bent fork, this segment of molding?*

No, she persisted, *not there.*

23.

Photographic fixer—used in the final step
of the process, the fixer stabilizes
the image against deterioration, against darkening.

IN DEFENSE OF NATURE POETRY

If you cry *get out of the woods*, the birds simply
move indoors. I say birds but we all picture
sparrows, those hearty little feather mice, fattened
on whatever their beaks will crack. In Shop-Rite,

they build nests of coupons, napkins, the spent tabs
of Band-Aids—I resist the urge to make a joke about
savings, nest egg—Anyway, there's no darkness
like a grocery store at night, just a sea of refrigeration cubes.

Day, darkness. Repeat, repeat. An egg laid, the little
hunger dreams of crickets miles off. And then there's
the fire escape gone fuzzy with ivy—this living thing
clinging to the inorganic. But I'm wrong again. Ivy

will climb whatever is closest, and this ladder's
made of metal, a substance found in the ground and
in the blood. As soon as it frosts, these leaves will
curl but refuse to fall. My body, too, is

governed by all kinds of laws. Every event in time just
a way of talking about space again. How much
we take up. So what's the use of a song with a birdbath, a
bank vault, a plant with metal limbs? We already have

something called the money tree. We already call
cash green. The sparrow triggers the automatic
door again—in and out—a blur of wing like a wisp
of hair, a keepsake—what we used to shut in

lockets to hold some loss. But I don't know
the first thing about survival, about treasures. I take
whatever catches the light and haul it home,
wide-eyed like a window that lets the snow right in.

INTERNAL REASONS AND THE OBSCURITY OF BLAME

I'm often sorry about wanting to catch you when you're down
      but other days I fake it. My work
requires some level of regret I can't muster consistently.

It rains. I open my heart enough to let a moth fly in,
      then trap it. I'm sorry to say that's how poems are made. One eye
on each wing, this whole-body blinking.

All of this makes sense as long as you keep yourself from thinking about it.
      Not an elephant. Not an oil crisis.

Until yesterday, several vials of smallpox remained
      unaccounted for, resting benevolent in a cardboard box
in an unused storage area of a research center in Bethesda.
      Concerning the accounted-for vials, those too
have yet to be destroyed by the United States
      or Russia.

It's easy to dream myself in a cardboard box. I'm
      very good at holding my breath.

But how can you not harbor doubts? Economist
      Morris Adelman died last month, his famous line—*We will never run out
of oil*. Or smallpox, as it happens.

As it happens, I go into the sunroom to water the jade, the child
      of my grandmother's plant which was cut
from her nurse's plant which was cut from her
      ex-husband's plant. I'm getting to the part where

I run out of things to say about extinction. Cut a branch
        and bury it. Sometimes
I'm sorry these plants take such little care, such
                little work required of me.

V.

THE GOLDEN RECORD

Diagram of a diagram: if properly decoded,

                    the first image which will appear

is a circle. Or, go backwards.

                The last image: a violin which, it seems,

can be read by music

               and is only the length of a sheet of paper

whatever a sheet of paper was

               in 1977. The year Jimmy Carter was elected.

———

The longest piece of music included is called,
in English, "Flowing Streams." Played
on the guqin, it slurs like the
human voice. Think: scale and silence, think:
vibrations and overtones, think: alone
in a desert carrying a very old instrument
swelling in the heat.

———

Image number 98: taken from inside the exhibit.

                 Foreground: elephant bones.

Large black rectangle symbolizing

                 museum glass, a thick frame, perhaps

bullet-proof and pressurized and

                 temperature-controlled to prevent

further decay.

———

Number 5: math   Number 8: math with colors   Number 105: a train with math

———

Jimmy Carter, remix:

We billion[s], we   likely, we
        rapidly hopeful   messages. Construct
survives any   attempt,   profoundly
        live, profoundly   altered.

This record is inhabited with   good will.

———

Pictured: cotton picker, grape picker, supermarket.
                                        Recall: touching all the fruit
        for ripeness. Recall:

                                        colonial exploit, strategic
        control. Whole lives spent plucking

                                        and spinning. The juice
        always so sweet against your teeth.

———

Pictured: the inside of a book on Newton.

                                        Nothing about gravity.
        Nothing like the stillness

                                        of the middle of a book
        cracked open like a locket.

———

Playback:

Images are made from signals. To render an image,
scan all 512 lines vertically and left to right.
8 milliseconds per line, 8 1/2 minutes per image.

———

Image number 17: Cell division magnified,
                              the lines clarifying, separating
their soft, rounded shapes.
                              These are most likely
human cells, most likely
                              benign.

———

Also in 1977, not pictured:
Apple Computers is incorporated; discovery of Legionnaire's disease; Elvis
Presley's last concert; *Star Wars* released in cinemas; U.S. park ranger Roy
Sullivan struck by lightning for the seventh time; snowfall in Miami for the
only time in recorded history—

———

Sounds from Earth: wild dog, tame dog.

———

Blues-gospel: "Dark was the night,
cold was the ground," a metaphor.

———

Greetings in 55 languages take 4 minutes and 14 seconds.
The time it takes to go to the end of the driveway, pick up
the newspaper, brush off leaves, go back inside and shut
the door.

The time it takes to steep chamomile tea.

———

Picture number 108: some kind of snow truck

                          attempting to cross

a deep ravine. Of course, it is also cold

                          in space and inside clouds

and in the holds of airplanes and

                          in the bottom of the ocean

but there isn't any snow out there.

                          This mutable substance—its melts,

its landscape on the landscape.

———

On the bottom, a pulsar map and Uranium-238. That static like a TV
no one ever unplugs, like at airport security—the sound of the wand waved over
your raised arms like a blessing. Recall also Hiroshima:

                          really big static. Definitely do not

look at that picture. Or, picture it in the background
with a small dog in the foreground or
don't take a picture to begin with.

                          Do not look back.

                          Do not disseminate.

                          Do not project into interstellar space.

———

As one track: volcano, earthquake, thunder

As one track: fire, speech

———

Of Beethoven's *Fifth*, only the first movement,
its opening a herald, the knock of fate. His three
other movements are left out, their systematic
fragmenting of the heroic theme.

———

The third to last picture:

a sunset with birds. Flying

north, or perhaps

south. Over the water, there is no

register of season, just

the sun, paused, a split

yolk on the horizon.

———

As one track: the first tools

———

As one track: Morse code between
ships: recall: states of emergency, recall:
The Titanic, onset of cold shock and
cardiac arrest—ice again. Bad analogy. Try:
the bleating of sheep, their dips and pauses, the
fuzz between radio stations, lamps that clap
on and off   on and off.

———

Jimmy Carter, in sequence:

The United States of America;

our message.

———

Pictured: The building that houses the United Nations
in daylight, then darkness.
When the sun hits
it is whole and smooth like a new book.

VI.

DARWINIST LOGIC ON HUMANITY

1. Most of our qualities are innate; nature triumphs over nurture.

It was Darwin's belief that our changeable hearts,
our persistent whimsy is nothing but a fallacy born
of shallow observation. Free will has been found
wanting, paper-thin, a ghost of the lazy intellect that
staunches curiosity, curbs an ugly existentialism.

They've been proving this with wolves. Raise a
domesticated dog in your house, a spaniel, and he
sleeps at the foot of your four-poster, sits where you
command he sit. Raise a wolf in your home and
he lies awake at night, running his tongue over his
sharpening teeth, chews the knobs off the
cabinets, eats all the bones from the trash, and stalks
the neighbors' pets, pushing his head into their cat
flaps and howling.

2. Humanity is not a natural or innate quality.

Perhaps this, too, is an accident of perception.
Underneath, there is a pattern, a clockwork of
subtle gears that approaches the appearance of a
needle on a moral compass: the swan floating
calmly on an undisturbed lake, yet pedaling
madly below the surface. Or it could be a rare gift
of chemical balance, that beautiful horizon where
insides and outsides align that disrupts the perfect
syllogism of genetic determination.

To prove this, we would need infinite time and
infinite objectivity, the ability to observe everyone
from beginning to end. We would need a supercomputer,
tallying yeses and noes, zeros and ones: *Does it
look like this? Like this? Like this? Like this?*

ARTIFACT (DISAMBIGUATION)

/ Object

Arrowheads in the streambed, box of photographs, rusted
nail. All must be buried & later exhumed when no one
needs to learn archery anymore (except to make
movies) & the people who might have known the people
in the photographs are dead & the nail just flakes to nothing. The role

of the artifact may be practical or symbolic, a result of the means
rather than the ends, i.e., collateral. As in software development: design
sketch or risk assessment, some tangible byproduct. As in science: a piece of hair
in a slide under a microscope bisecting the cells of an orchid petal or
the emergence of dog-like traits in the silver fox when
successively bred for tameness.

ARTIFACT (DISAMBIGUATION)

/ Error

Echoes, or pre-echoes introduced by the equipment or
techniques involved. Also called ghosts, like ghost in the machine, but we
are actually talking about machines this time like
when you adjust your car radio & it whistles or rattles or warbles or
sounds like you are suddenly underwater & you tilt your
head like a few drops might just spill out onto the seat. In this way,

offending artifacts may obscure, distort or completely
misrepresent. As in digital imaging: the rainbow
effect, the silk-screen effect, the screen-door effect, purple fringing. Or,
more gravely, iatrogenic artifacts, e.g., misrepresentations of tissue structures,
the lung or the breast too grainy or too cloudy or too dark or too soft.

ARTIFACTS, HANDLING

All artifacts are extremely fragile even when they do not appear so.

The best preservation practice would be to hold them in complete darkness.

ARTIFACT (DISAMBIGUATION)

/ In Popular Culture

A trading card in the game *Magic: The Gathering*; a science fiction novel by Gregory Benford; a documentary film directed by Jared Leto under the pseudonym Bartholomew Cubbins; a fictional object appearing on the TV series *Eureka*; a hip-hop duo from New Jersey; an album of ambient music by American artist Steve Roach; in fantasy, an object whose magical powers are so potent it cannot be duplicated or destroyed by ordinary means.

DARWIN (DISAMBIGUATION)

An early sign of Darwinism is a penchant
for collecting. In extreme cases, the child can think of little
but buttons or bottle caps. From a certain angle,
this collection will appear to be a veiled obsession
with death, each thing carefully removed from its context, arranged

and preserved with its like kind. Darwin himself began
with matches, but quickly turned to insects, despite
the great chagrin of his peers. He was insufferable on a hunt,
constantly stopping to collect new specimens. Once, two rare beetles
in each fist, he spotted another at the base of a young oak. Overcome,

Charlie popped one into his mouth to take hold of the precious third.
Even those of us who are not collectors might recognize
this moment, in which the beetle scrabbling furiously against his upper canines
is the only thing one can now hope to save.

ARTIFACT (DISAMBIGUATION)

/ See Also

Artifact Puzzles, including the 1,000-piece jigsaw of a Boeing
747 laser-cut in nontraditional style, shapes like Greek
letters & bird feet. Then there is the Artifact-Centric Business Process
Model & the self-consuming artifact, a term coined by Stanley Fish
to describe an effect of rhetoric in which a textual structure
points to its own shortcomings, to something it cannot capture. See

also: OOPArt, short for Out-of-Place Artifacts, which appear to
demonstrate human presence in historical, archaeological, or
paleontological contexts that would otherwise seem impossible. These
are artifacts twice-over being both errors & objects, e.g., The Dendera
Lamps, stone reliefs carved in Ptolemaic Egypt that closely resemble
lightbulbs, & Piri Reis, whose map showed Antarctica before
it was discovered. Both fall under the category: unlikely interpretations. Other
categories: unusual, questionable & erroneously dated, e.g., The Calaveras
Skull, an admitted hoax. See also: *Book of Artifacts*, the supplemental
sourcebook for the Advanced Dungeons & Dragons role-playing game, e.g.,
Queen Ehlissa's Marvelous Nightingale, which is at least partially clockwork but
animate. It emits brilliant light from its eyes, restoring lost
energy. Those who keep it never hunger or thirst.

NOTES ON RELIEF

from the journal of an amateur genealogist

I.
You could say I suffer from
long-range determinism. I think a lot about
passenger pigeons, trying
to suss out possible ties—one century
the most abundant bird in the world and
the next, extinct.

At 10 in the morning, I'm already on Untitled Document 26.

2.
There's something mosquitoes love about
girls, as if they can smell the extra blood. Type O
tastes best of all but who knows why. A rare commodity then,
my sweetness.

In high school, the Red Cross came looking
for donations. I weighed too little to give any.
And I was proud of it.

This is really what girls are like.

3.
Last year, an important breakthrough was made
on the subject of itching. Hello
little neuropeptides, found you at last. But this discovery
taught us nothing about the feeling that comes
when you scratch and scratch, what tells the brain

right there, you got it, right there, yes—

4.
My father is O also and donates often to keep
his cholesterol down.

5.
Darwin's father, a doctor, opposed the practice
of bleeding patients though it remained prevalent
throughout his lifetime.

(As were the passenger pigeons, on another continent,
flying overhead in flocks of billions.)

For the most part, Dr. Darwin just talked to people,
tried to help them understand lineage. Yes, the passenger pigeon

was thought to be most closely related
to the mourning dove, but it was a false symbolism, their
mourning—more beautiful than true.

6.
An excess of meaning in their name also—from the French
    passager, to pass by.

It scratches an itch, certainly.

7.
Inside this quiet I find there is
a smaller one rarely reached and thus
sweetest of all.

SALT (DISAMBIGUATION)

Too much or too little—both
are fatal, they say. I spend these days trying to grow something with edges

in the dark that sits at the back of my brain. I wash my face, push
static into the crevice at the corner of each eye.
Other salt: in rocks, in water, in pills, in blood. In cryptography,

a salt is an input used to defend against dictionary hacks. I don't think
I'm making myself clear. What aren't we trying
                                        to preserve? Yes,

if you have the choice, paint the door red. In some cultures,
        it brings luck. Behind the door, a stack of letters from an ex
written in transit—his shaky hand. Salt (software): the grains

constitute a system for detecting and storing static information for rapid
        access. This is not what you'd call fieldwork.
                                        Rather, the only time

we ever went to my parents' house, he went for a long walk alone, his
        phone face down on the mattress. Syntactic salt (in programming): to prevent
against bad code.
                On the sidewalk, a smashed cricket, ants

        fighting over its sweetness. Syntactic sugar: gratuitous syntax
that refuses to simplify. There are all kinds of things I own whose use
        is compromised by aesthetics—a set of silver

fish knives in their velvet-lined box. I need
        some proof of loss—salt in the wound—He walked
all the way to the Hudson, returned with pockets full of rocks. Funny how beautiful

they seem when wet. An estuary, the ocean pushing upstream—
        it refuses to freeze. Each flake of snow
shattering against the surface, hundreds of them, the sound

like stroking fur backwards, against the eagerness of all things
        to dissolve, to cohere.

NOTES

I.

"Terrifying Robot Update": For Marty Weishaar. The Wormwood Forest surrounding the Chernobyl Nuclear Plant became known as the Red Forest after radiation killed the pines, leaving acres of ginger-brown branches. The title comes from a Tumblr by the same name.

"Nine Ways in which Pac-Man Speaks to the Human Condition": For Abe Barth-Werb, who showed me Jonathan Blow's lecture on video games and the human condition. As for the Middlemist Camellia, there are two known specimens remaining in the world.

"Correction: Tonight Is Not the Longest Night in the History of Earth": Special thanks to Jenny Boychuk for linking me to the article from which this title derives, originally posted and then revised the following day by Joseph Stromberg for *Vox*. The night in question was the 2014 winter solstice. Thanks to Annie Bolotin for the Sleep Cycle app and to Frank O'Hara for "pain produces logic."

"Eight years ago,": For Alex Willingham, for continuing to run SETI@home and contributing to the search for whatever might be out there. The Cambodian temple referred to here is Boeng Mealea, now a UNESCO World Heritage Site.

II.

"Darwin (disambiguation)": From Darwin's autobiography: "as a little boy I was much given to inventing deliberate falsehoods, and this was always done for the sake of causing excitement."

"When I Ask the Internet If the Sun Is a Ball of Fire": For Lauren Prastien. In the original Pokémon Red game, Pokémon that sustain burns in battle continue to lose health even after the battle ends until the player applies an item called "Burn Heal." This is in contrast to most other attacks, which reduce a Pokémon's health only once.

"If Not for the Intervention of Man, or Darwinist Logic on Freebies": The robot in rain boots refers to hitchBOT. Designed by Dr. David Smith and Dr. Frauke Zeller, hitchBOT hitched a total of 19 rides from Halifax, Nova Scotia to Victoria, British Columbia in the summer of 2014. Thanks to Colin Welch for introducing me to the chatbot chatter on Twitter referenced here, in which three bots, @oliviataters, @notkeithcalder, and @BofA_Help conversed independently of humans on issues of love, banking assistance, and popular television.

"Darwinist Logic on Pattern Recognition": The blight referenced here is the chestnut blight *Cryphonectria parasitica*, a pathogenic fungus that devastated the American chestnut population in the eastern United States in the first half of the twentieth century. Leaves of the chestnut tree turn yellow in Autumn; leaves of the chestnut oak turn red.

"Red, Save!": For all the Willinghams. Originally released in North America in 1998, Pokémon Red was played by thousands simultaneously in 2014 via the streaming service Twitch.tv, which hosted a video stream of the game while simultaneously parsing commands sent by users via the channel's chat room. The game was completed after more than sixteen days of continuous gameplay. A speed run by an individual takes just under two hours.

III.

"Darwinist Logic on Unrequited Love": For Adeeba Talukder.

"Let's Hope Kepler-186f Is Barren": For Kat Finch. The title comes from Andrew Snyder-Beattie's article on the Fermi paradox published in *Ars Technica*.

"Darwinist Logic on Disappointment": For Ryan Dzelzkalns. Darwin's health issues were complex enough that they occupy a Wikipedia page of their own. His uncommon combination of symptoms left him debilitated for long periods and remained undiagnosed in his lifetime. Later hypotheses include various chronic neuroses and immune disorders or parasites such as panic disorder, psychosomatic disorder, obsessive-compulsive disorder, Crohn's disease, Ménière's disease, Lupus erythematosus, cyclic vomiting syndrome, chronic fatigue syndrome, or, one of the most popular theories, Chagas disease, believed to have been contracted from certain South American insects he studied, though evidences against this hypothesis are equally numerous. Darwin's children suffered from similarly vague illnesses in their early years, leading Darwin to fear he had passed on some hereditary condition, though again it remains impossible to confirm this.

"Bad Instructions for Approaching Warp Speed": Zoë Quinn is a video game developer whose home address was discovered in the process of a massive harassment campaign stemming from what's now known as the GamerGate controversy. Thanks to Aryeh Gold-Parker for sending me the photographic postcard of "Ansel Adams Photographing in Yosemite Valley" taken by Cedric Wright in 1946.

"Whatever": For Kaija Bergen. The insect referenced here is the planthopper, whose back legs contain the first mechanical gear system ever observed in nature. The repeated phrase is from Eminem's hit song "The Way I Am" recorded in 2000.

IV.

"Dear Charlie": Thanks to Lorna Goodison for introducing me to her husband J. Edward Chamberlin's work on Darwin's relationship to our understanding of islands. The robots mentioned here refer to those in the 1986 Studio Ghibli film *Castle in the Sky* written and directed by Hayao Miyazaki.

"Twitch (disambiguation)": Twitch gameplay refers to scenarios in video games that test a player's reaction time. Twitch gameplay is not normally a prominent feature of Pokémon Red but it was an important element to the meta-game of Twitch Plays Pokémon where users needed to react to the command inputs coming through from thousands of other players.

"A Partial List of Overwriting Errors": Thanks to H. R. Webster for linking me to Marius, the eighteen-month-old giraffe referenced here who was killed at Copenhagen zoo on February 9, 2014 because his genes were too common to breed. The rock formation described here is known as the "Face on Mars" and was first recorded by the Viking 1 in 1976 while photographing the Cydonia region of Mars. The black marks dotting the surface are a result of data errors.

"Internal Reasons and the Obscurity of Blame": Thanks to Larisa Svirsky for this title, which comes from a philosophy paper by Bernard Williams published in 1989. The World Health Organization has been calling for destruction of remaining stocks of the smallpox virus since 1986 but has been repeatedly met with resistance by the United States and Russia. Although some scientists argue that holding on to small stocks could be useful in developing vaccines or anti-viral drugs, a review conducted by the WHO concluded in 2010 that no essential public health purpose is served by retaining stocks of this virus.

V.

"The Golden Record": The title and contents of this piece refer to the phonograph disc containing images and sounds chosen to represent humanity on the Voyager 1 Spacecraft launched in 1977. Among other things, the poem contains a "remix" of Jimmy Carter's message included on the record.

VI.

"Artifacts, handling": Adapted from the Texas Historical Commission's "Basic Guidelines for the Preservation of Historic Artifacts," 2013.

"Darwin (disambiguation)": Darwin himself recounts this story in his autobiography as "proof of my zeal." Unfortunately, the insect he placed in his mouth for safekeeping caused trouble: "Alas it ejected some intensely acrid fluid, which burnt my tongue so that I was forced to spit the beetle out, which was lost, as well as the third one."

———

"Notes on Relief": The neuropeptide referenced here is natriuretic polypeptide b, which was discovered to be specific to the sensation of itching in a study by Santosh Mishra and Mark Hoon published in 2013. With regards to the passenger pigeon, genetic analysis conducted in 2010 concluded that the species is most closely related to the American *Patagioenas* pigeons, located in a different clade of pigeons altogether from the mourning dove.